Monuments to Remember

Samantha Bell

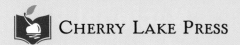

Published in the United States of America by Cherry Lake Publishing Group
Ann Arbor, Michigan
www.cherrylakepublishing.com

Reading Adviser: Beth Walker Gambro, MS, Ed., Reading Consultant, Yorkville, IL

Photo Credits: cover, title page: © Sebastien Burel/Shutterstock; page 4: NPS/Terry Adams; page 5: NPS Photo; page 7: © Thanasis F/Shutterstock; page 8: © TZIDO SUN/Shutterstock; page 11: © eurobanks/Shutterstock; page 12: © Jerry Coli/Dreamstime.com; page 13: © TempleNick/Shutterstock; page 14: NPS / Victoria Stauffenberg; page 15: © Patricia A Hamilton/Dreamstime.com; page 17: NPS Photo; page 18: © KMarsh/Shutterstock; page 21: NPS Photo; page 22: NPS/Tim Ertel; page 23: © Jon Bilous/Shutterstock; page 24: © Joe Sohm/Dreamstime.com; page 25: NPS Photo/Fort McHenry social media team; page 27: The George F. Landegger Collection of Alabama Photographs in Carol M. Highsmith's America, Library of Congress, Prints and Photographs Division; page 29: Trikosko, Marion S., photographer, U.S. News & World Report Magazine Photograph Collection, Library of Congress, Prints and Photographs Division; page 30: © GaudiLab/Shutterstock

Cherry Lake Press is an imprint of Cherry Lake Publishing Group.

Library of Congress Cataloging-in-Publication Data

Names: Bell, Samantha, author.
Title: Monuments to remember / written by Samantha Bell.
Description: Ann Arbor, Michigan : Cherry Lake Publishing, [2024] | Series: National park adventures | Includes bibliographical references and index. | Audience: Grades 4-6 | Summary: "Visit the sculptures and memorials that preserve our nation's memory. Rising at the center of the National Mall, the Washington Monument is just one of the sculptures and structures built to honor our nation's shared past. Part of our 21st Century Skills Library, this series introduces concepts of natural sciences and social studies centered around a sense of adventure"— Provided by publisher.
Identifiers: LCCN 2023010573 | ISBN 9781668927441 (hardcover) | ISBN 9781668928493 (paperback) | ISBN 9781668929964 (ebook) | ISBN 9781668931448 (pdf)
Subjects: LCSH: National monuments—United States—Juvenile literature.
Classification: LCC E159 .B413 2024 | DDC 973—dc23/eng/20230331
LC record available at https://lccn.loc.gov/2023010573

Cherry Lake Publishing Group would like to acknowledge the work of the Partnership for 21st Century Learning, a Network of Battelle for Kids. Please visit http://www.battelleforkids.org/networks/p21 for more information.

Printed in the United States of America
Corporate Graphics

Note from publisher: Websites change regularly, and their future contents are outside of our control. Supervise children when conducting any recommended online searches for extended learning opportunities.

Samantha Bell was born and raised near Orlando, Florida. She grew up in a family of eight kids and all kinds of pets, including goats, chickens, cats, dogs, rabbits, horses, parakeets, hamsters, guinea pigs, a monkey, a raccoon, and a coatimundi. She now lives with her family in the foothills of the Blue Ridge Mountains, where she enjoys hiking, painting, and snuggling with their cats Pocket, Pebble, and Mr. Tree-Tree Triggers.

CONTENTS

Introduction

National monuments are not only natural objects or places. They can also be structures, sculptures, and places with historical and cultural value. The monuments preserve these sites. That way, people will be able to visit and learn about them for years to come. Only Congress can create a national park. But any president can establish a national monument.

CHAPTER 1

Statue of Liberty National Monument

New York City, New York

One of the most well-known national monuments stands in New York City's harbor. The Statue of Liberty is a **symbol** of freedom and opportunity. It stands 305 feet (93 meters) tall, from the ground up to the tip of the torch. It was dedicated on October 28, 1886. The statue of a woman called Lady Liberty was a gift of friendship from the people of France. It was designed with many symbols of freedom. The book the statue carries has the date the Declaration of Independence was signed. Her feet are marching, leading the way to freedom. The broken chain and shackle at her foot celebrates the end of slavery.

The Statue of Liberty was a gift from France.

Lady Liberty welcomed immigrants into New York Harbor when they traveled through to Ellis Island between 1892 and 1954.

Before 1890, individual states handled **immigration**. But as the number of immigrants increased, this became more difficult. Instead, the U.S. government established Ellis Island. Here, immigrants had their health and documents inspected. From 1892 to 1954, more than 12 million immigrants came through Ellis Island. The first thing they saw when they arrived at the harbor was the Statue of Liberty. For many, it was a very emotional moment. The statue represented their new start in a free land.

Both the Statue of Liberty and Ellis Island are part of the Statue of Liberty National Monument. They help preserve the memories and stories of the immigrants who came for a better life. Visitors may take tours of Liberty Island and the Statue of Liberty. They can view exhibits inside the statue's pedestal. Then they can take an elevator to the pedestal observatory. The observatory offers full-circle views of New York Harbor and a close-up look at the statue. Visitors can climb a spiral staircase to the crown. At Ellis Island, they can tour the museum. They can also search for their family history.

SHINING A NEW LIGHT

Visitors to the Statue of Liberty used to be able to go to the balcony of the torch. But during World War I (1914–1918), German spies planted explosives at a **munitions depot** in New York Harbor. The United States used the depot to send ammunition to the Allied forces in Europe. The explosion caused **debris** that damaged the statue's arm and torch. They were finally repaired in 1984. The torch was replaced with a new one. The original torch is in the pedestal museum.

CHAPTER 2

National Mall

Washington, D.C.

The National Mall is often called "America's Front Yard." It is located in the country's capital. The mall stretches more than 2 miles (3.2 kilometers) from the Lincoln Memorial on the west end to the U.S. Capitol on the east end. It has more than 100 memorials and museums. Some of them honor important historical figures. Others honor Americans who died in service to the country. The National Mall is the most visited national park. People come to learn about the nation's history and **heritage**.

The annual Blossom Kite Festival at the Cherry Blossom Festival on the National Mall

Some of the monuments and memorials honor past presidents. The Washington Monument was built to honor the first president. It is the shape of an Egyptian **obelisk**. It stands 555 feet (169 meters) high in the center of the mall. The Lincoln Memorial is on the western end of the mall. It was created to honor President Abraham Lincoln. The design was inspired by ancient Greek temples. It has 36 columns. Each one represents a state at the time of Lincoln's death. Inside is a 19-foot (5.8 m) statue of Lincoln. Other memorials that honor presidents include the Thomas Jefferson Memorial, the Ulysses S. Grant Memorial, and the Franklin Delano Roosevelt Memorial.

The cherry trees on the National Mall were originally donated by Tokyo, Japan to the United States in 1909. You can see the Washington Monument above the trees.

The Atlantic entrance to the World War II
Memorial on the National Mall

Some memorials honor those who fought for freedom. The Vietnam Veterans Memorial honors those who fought in the war. It features a wall with the names of 58,318 Americans who died in the war. Visitors to this memorial leave mementos, letters, and photographs of loved ones they lost. The National World War II Memorial honors the men and women who served and the thousands who died. Other war memorials on the mall include the District of Columbia War Memorial and the Korean War Veterans Memorial.

A WAY TO REMEMBER

Most of the memorials on the National Mall honor presidents or veterans. But a few memorials honor private citizens. The Martin Luther King, Jr. Memorial features a 30-foot (9 m) statue of King carved from a block of stone. The John Ericsson Memorial honors the designer of the Union warship, the *USS Monitor*. John Paul Jones was a naval hero during the Revolutionary War (1775-1783). He has a statue on the mall. George Mason was a **Founding Father**. He has a memorial on the mall, too.

CHAPTER 3

African Burial Ground National Monument

New York City, New York

In 1991, construction began on a new office building in New York City. First, archeologists had to **excavate** the area. Many were shocked at what they found. They uncovered the skeletal remains of 419 enslaved and free Africans. It was one small part of a 6-acre (2.4 hectares) burial ground. The burial ground stretched across five city blocks. Archeologists believe that approximately 15,000 enslaved and free Africans were buried here. They had lived and worked in New York when it was still a colony.

This sculpture by Barbara Chase-Riboud at the African Burial Ground National Monument is called *Africa Rising*.

A view of part of the African Burial Ground National Monument in New York

The discovery changed the way people viewed the construction of New York City. The city began as a settlement in 1624. It had fewer than 300 people. By 1760, it had a population of 18,000. New York had become the second-largest city in the colonies. The burial ground was used from the middle 1630s until 1795. These are the same years the city was growing. It meant enslaved Africans were helping to build the city. Historians did not realize that so many enslaved people had a part in it.

In 1997, a contest was held to create a memorial for the Burial Ground. The winning design included a lot of symbolism. The **granite** structure at the site is called the Ancestral Chamber. It represents the front of the slave ships. These ships carried thousands of Africans to North America. The Chamber has a doorway people can walk through. It leads to a dark and narrow space. This symbolizes the part of the journey on the ships. Enslaved people spent months crammed into small spaces. At the chamber, visitors can hear the sound of rushing water. Other symbols along the wall represent the different African cultures and people who were enslaved.

SAYING GOODBYE

When Africans died, they were not allowed to be buried in the church graveyards in the city. Instead, African people developed the burial ground. At the time, it was outside the fence that surrounded the city. Africans in the colony also faced other restrictions. No more than 12 people could be in a funeral procession. Only 12 could be at a graveside service, too. They could not hold funeral services at night. Night burials were an African custom. People were not allowed to practice their beliefs. As the population of enslaved people grew, the burial ground grew, too. They began to run out of room. They had to stack some of the coffins on top of each other.

CHAPTER 4

Fort McHenry National Monument and Historic Shrine

Baltimore, Maryland

Baltimore Harbor connects the city of Baltimore with the Chesapeake Bay. During the American Revolution, a small fort was built near the harbor. It was called Fort Whetstone. The fort protected Baltimore. It was the country's third-largest city at the time. In 1798, the fort was expanded. It was renamed Fort McHenry. In the years that followed, the British tried to control American trade with other countries. They forced American sailors to join their navy. In 1812, the United States declared war on England.

Historical reenactors play drums in the Fort McHenry courtyard.

The interior of Fort McHenry is laid out in the shape of a pentagon.

The next year, the British entered Chesapeake Bay. By August 1814, they had captured and burned down Washington, D.C.

Next, the British decided to attack Baltimore. On September 13, 1814, 5,000 British soldiers landed near the city. The British Navy would attack from the harbor. One thousand defenders waited for them at Fort McHenry. The British Navy began shooting bombs and rockets. They fired at the fort for 25 hours. A lawyer named Francis Scott Key witnessed the attack. He waited for the fog and smoke to clear. Then he saw the American flag still flying over the fort. He knew the Americans had won. He was so inspired that he wrote a poem. He called it "The Defense of Fort McHenry." The words were later put to music. It was renamed "The Star-Spangled Banner." It became the country's national anthem.

A NEW PURPOSE

After the War of 1812, Fort McHenry was never attacked again. However, it remained an active military post for many years. During the Civil War, it continued to defend Baltimore Harbor. It was also used as a prison for Confederate soldiers. But during World War I (1914–1918), it was given a new purpose. A hospital was constructed around the fort. It was used to treat wounded or sick soldiers coming back from the **front**. During that time, Fort McHenry became known as General Hospital No. 2. It was the busiest time in the fort's history.

The American flag flies over Fort McHenry.

The evening flag change at Fort McHenry

The fort is now a national monument. It is one of the most popular tourist spots in Baltimore. Visitors can tour the fort and learn more about its history. Every morning and evening, rangers change the flag. In the evening, they raise a modern American flag. In the mornings, they raise a copy of a historic flag. Rangers have a large collection of flags to choose from. They are different sizes. The flag they choose usually depends on the weather. The largest flag is 42-foot by 30-foot (13 meters by 9 meters). Visitors to the fort often help change the flags.

CHAPTER 5

Birmingham Civil Rights National Monument

Birmingham, Alabama

Birmingham, Alabama was once one of the most segregated U.S. cities. After the Civil War and the Compromise of 1877, laws separated Black and White people. In many places like Alabama, Black people could not drink from the same water fountains as White people. They could not go to the same parks or use the same elevators. They could not swim in the same pools. Black people worked hard against inequality. They did this for many years. In the 1950s and 1960s, the civil rights movement gained more and more support. People gathered for **nonviolent protests**. Hundreds of marchers filled the streets. They sat in places reserved for White people only. Leaders such as Dr. Martin Luther King Jr.

The bombing of the 16th Street Baptist Church contributed greatly to the passage of the Civil Rights Act of 1964.

Many protesters lost their jobs. Police officers and firemen attacked protesters. They sprayed protesters with **water cannons**. They attacked them with police dogs as well. They arrested many protesters. One of Dr. King's most famous letters was written from a Birmingham jail. In all, 60 Black homes, businesses, and churches were bombed. Alabama's governor, George Wallace, even promised to defend segregation. The world watched as Black people continued to stand for freedom and justice. Then in September 1963, the 16th Street Baptist Church was bombed. Four young Black girls died. The tragic event contributed greatly to the passage of the Civil Rights Act of 1964. This law makes it illegal to discriminate against someone based on their race or skin color.

SEEING HISTORY

Kelly Ingram Park contains several statues honoring the civil rights movement. In the center of the park is a statue of Martin Luther King Jr. Another statue recreates a famous photo from 1960. A police officer is grabbing a young Black man by his shirt. A dog is lunging at the man. Other sculptures depict children in jail or being hit by water cannons. Another sculpture is of the four girls killed in the church bombing. One girl is releasing six doves. They represent the four girls and two others who were killed later that day.

The A.G. Gaston Motel served as a meeting place for many civil rights activists. Martin Luther King Jr. is pictured here on its balcony in 1963.

The Birmingham Civil Rights National Monument site was established to remember the work of the civil rights movement. It includes various buildings in the Historic Birmingham Civil Rights District. One of these is the A.G. Gaston Motel. Established in 1954, the hotel was owned by a Black man named George Gaston. It served as a base for many civil rights activists. Another site is Kelly Ingram Park. Civil rights protesters gathered in this park in 1963. Sometimes police officers broke up their protests with violence. The 16th Street Baptist Church is also part of the monument.

Activity

Plan Your Adventure!

There are many national monuments that help us remember important times in American history. Is there an event or person you would like to learn about? Check to see if there is a monument you can visit to find out more. Then look through the other books in this series to discover even more things to see, do, and learn about in the national parks.

Design a Monument

The monuments in this book were created to remember a certain person, place, or event in U.S. history. Many are designed using symbols, such as the columns at the Lincoln Memorial or the Ancestral Chamber at the African Burial Ground. Think of a place or event that is important to you. On a piece of paper, design a monument that represents that place or event. Include symbols on your monument. Then write a short paragraph describing what your monument represents and what the symbols mean. Be sure to tell where you would put your monument and why.

Learn More

Books

Daigneau, Jean. *Ellis Island and Immigration for Kids: A History with 21 Activities.* Chicago, IL: Chicago Review Press, 2021.

Kallio, Jamie. *The National Mall.* Edina, MN: ABDO Publishing, 2020.

Mattern, Joanne. *Fort McHenry: Our Flag was Still There.* South Egremont, MA: Red Chair Press, 2018.

Walker, Cameron. *National Monuments of the USA.* London, UK: Wide Eyed Editions, 2023.

On the Web

With an adult, learn more online with these suggested searches.

"Ellis Island Expedition Series." National Park Service.

"Fort McHenry Virtual Tour." National Park Service.

"Lincoln Memorial Centennial Virtual Field Trip." Trust for the National Mall.

"Statue of Liberty." National Geographic Kids.

Glossary

debris (duh-BREE) scattered pieces left after something has been destroyed

excavate (EK-skuh-vayt) to dig something out

Founding Father (FOUN-ding FAH-thur) one of the American Revolution leaders who helped unite the colonies and create a new government

front (FRUHNT) the place in war where the heaviest fighting occurs

granite (GRAH-nuht) a hard stone used for making buildings, monuments, and sculptures

heritage (HAYR-uh-tij) traditions, monuments, and culture passed down from one generation to another

immigration (ih-muh-GRAY-shuhn) the act of moving from one's home country to another land

munitions depot (myoo-NIH-shuhns DEE-poh) a military storage place for ammunition

nonviolent protests (nahn-VYE-uh-luhnt PROH-tests) ways to bring about change without hurting anyone or causing damage

obelisk (AH-buh-lisk) a pillar that tapers and ends in a pyramid shape

symbol (SIM-buhl) marks or objects that represent something else

water cannons (WAH-tuhr KAH-nuhnz) devices that send out a powerful jet of water

Index